Collins

EXPLORE ENGLISH

Student's Resource Book 5

Contents

About this book

This book is full of interesting texts for you to enjoy.

- You can read and discuss **stories.**

- You can read **information** about people, places and animals.

Takumi needs time
Takumi works in Tokyo and it takes him 55 minutes to get to work.

Hello Bo! How's was your trip to the Drakensberg? It was GREAT!

- There are **poems** to read aloud, perform and enjoy.

This tells you there is something to **talk** about.

When Sarah Surfs the Internet
When Sarah surfs the internet she starts by checking mail. She answers all her messages from friends in great detail.

This tells you there is something to **think** about.

Enjoy the book!

I'm pleased to meet you

Read these introductions to find out about people who live in different parts of the world.

Maria's story

Kamusta, I'm Maria!

I was born on the beautiful island of Cebu, in the Philippines. I have two older brothers and we live with my mum just 100 m from the beach.

I attend Sun Coast Primary School and enjoy science the most because my teacher is really funny. I love surfing with my friends on the weekends. I dislike rainy days because I can't go outside to play.

Bolin's story

Nǐ hǎo, I'm Bolin!

I'm from China, but now I live in England in a homestay. This means that I am living with a British family in London. They look after me while I attend high school and practise English. My real mum and dad live in Shanghai, China. I'm an only child – I don't have any brothers or sisters.

I have many hobbies. I love reading history books and building my own mini robots. I also enjoy playing in the local basketball team.

Amira and Ashira's story

Salam, I'm Amira and this is my sister, Ashira!

We are twins from the city of Islamabad in Pakistan. We're both seven years old and have just started school. We live with our parents and one older brother who always teases us.

My name means 'princess' in English. Sometimes my dad calls me princess to make me laugh. I laugh a lot! I love playing outside, eating sweet things and wearing pink. My sister also loves playing outside, but she hates pink. We love to go to the park together after school to play with our friends.

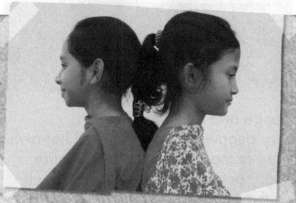

João's story

Olá, I'm João!

I'm Brazilian. I'm in Grade 6. I am tall and strong and I play many sports. I am the captain of my school's soccer team. My name is 'John' in English.

Even though I live near the sea, I don't enjoy swimming. I prefer walking in the mountains or flying my kite. I made my own kite last year. It is red, orange and yellow, like fire.

Siyabonga's story

Molo, I'm Siyabonga!

I'm from Cape Town, South Africa. I live with my mum dad, sister and grandmother.

I am interested in reading, taking photos and drawing pictures. I can run really fast! Last year, I won all the races at my school.

When I finish my homework, I spend time writing. I have almost finished writing my first storybook. It is about three cats that get lost and have to find their way home. I also drew all my own pictures for the story. One day, I hope to be a famous writer.

Which things would you talk about if you introduced yourself?

We can make the world awesome

Listen to this short talk about Katie Stagliano.

Katie's Krops

This is Katie Stagliano. She comes from South Carolina, USA. When she was in third grade, she planted a cabbage seedling. It grew and grew and grew until it finally weighed 18 kg! Katie knew this cabbage was special, so she donated it to a soup kitchen. It was made into soup and helped feed over 275 people.

Katie felt good about donating her cabbage and decided to plant a vegetable patch to help feed more hungry people. At first, she used her own garden. Then, she started using some land at the school. More and more people joined Katie's dream to feed hungry people. She now has her own company called Katie's Krops with more than 80 gardens!

All of these gardens are growing vegetables for the needy. Many people volunteer their time to work in the gardens and help cook food with the vegetables. Katie even wrote a book about her first cabbage, called *Katie's Cabbage*. If Katie could do so much good when she was only nine years old, then surely we could all find a way to help people who have less than we do.

How can you help less fortunate people?

Who are we   Watch videos   The blog   Buy stuff   Contact Brad

KID PRESIDENT

This is Robby Novak, also known as 'Kid President'. He was born in 2004 with osteogenesis imperfecta. This means that his bones break easily. In fact, Robby has broken his bones more than 70 times! But this hasn't stopped him from working hard towards his goals.

Robby has a dream. He wants the world to be a better place. He wants people to be happy and to love each other. So, Robby started a YouTube channel with his brother-in-law, Brad Montague. People loved their videos, and soon they became an internet sensation!

They have made over 100 videos and have received more than 50 millions views. They have also written a book together and created a website. Their book is called *Kid President's Guide to Being Awesome*.

People love Robby's sense of humour and positive attitude. He teaches people to respect each other. He says that we should all work together to make the world better – to fill it with love, to end global problems and to fix our planet. He believes that wherever you are, you have everything you need to make the world awesome!

How can you make the world awesome?

Plan to achieve

Ten steps to achieve your goals

1 Dare to dream
Think about the future.
What is important to you?
What do you want to achieve?

2 Write it down
Put your dream into words.
Display it where you can
see it every day.

4 Create a 'goal ladder'
Make a list of smaller goals.
Each step should show a small
goal you need to achieve so
that you can finally achieve
your big goal.

3 Check that your goal is 'SMART'
Your goal should be:
Specific,
Measureable,
Attainable, Relevant
and Time-bound.

Goal setting	
S	Specific
M	Measurable
A	Attainable
R	Relevant
T	Time-bound

5 Create deadlines
When do you want to
achieve your goal?
Make a deadline for
your big goal.
Then, make deadlines
for your smaller goals.

6 Collect what you need
Most goals need some resources.
Make a list of what you need.
Then start collecting those things.

7 Go for it!
The best time to start achieving
your goal is right now!

8 Track your progress
As you achieve each small
goal, tick it off your list.

10 Celebrate your success!
Celebrate every small goal
you achieve.

9 Never give up
Because successful people
never, ever give up!

Which is the most
important step? Which is
the least important step?

Asking questions

Read this interview with Bolin.

Interviewee

Interviewer

Interviewer: Hi, Bolin! It is good to meet you. How are you today?

Bolin: I'm very well, thank you. And you?

Interviewer: I'm great. I'm also excited to learn more about you. Where do you come from?

Bolin: I come from Shanghai, China.

Interviewer: How long ago did you move to London?

Bolin: I moved here two years ago.

Interviewer: Why did you move to London?

Bolin: I moved here to learn English and to experience life in a different country.

Interviewer: Whose idea was that?

Bolin: It was my father's idea.

Interviewer: Are you happy that you moved here?

Bolin: Oh, yes! In the beginning it was difficult. I was very lonely but now I have many friends. I love my school and my hobbies.

Interviewer: Which hobbies do you enjoy?

Bolin: Wow, I have so many! I love reading, especially about Chinese history. I also love building robots. When it's sunny, I love doing sports outside, meeting my friends and just relaxing, of course.

Interviewer: What is your dream for the future?

Bolin: I hope to return to China after university. I want to teach English to people in the small villages. One day, I hope to open a school that teaches English and computer skills in rural China.

Interviewer: That's incredible! I wish you all the best for achieving your dream.

Bolin: Thank you very much.

How long?   Where?

How many?

How?

How many question words can you find in the interview?

Where are you from?

Why?   HOW OFTEN?   Which?

What do you enjoy doing?   Whose?   **What are your dreams?**

Which questions work?

Read this interview with Maria.

Interviewer: Good morning, Maria. Welcome to this interview.

Maria: Good morning to you too. Thank you very much. I am happy to be here.

Interviewer: You are from Cebu, right?

Maria: Yes, that's right.

Interviewer: That's in the Philippines, isn't it?

Maria: Yes, it is.

Interviewer: Please tell us more about Cebu.

Maria: Sure, Cebu is actually a big island, with more than 100 small islands around it. All the beaches are beautiful. The sand is white and the sea is clear. Many tourists visit Cebu to relax and see the beautiful area.

Interviewer: Wow, it sounds incredible! What do you like doing in your free time?

Maria: I really love surfing! My mum calls me 'surf-baby'.

Interviewer: How often do you surf?

Maria: I surf every day after school.

Interviewer: Do you have a dream for your future?

Maria: Yes! My dream is to travel the world! I want to surf in many different places – Hawaii, South Africa, Thailand, Mexico, Australia ... everywhere!

Interviewer: Wow, that's fantastic! Good luck for your future. I hope your dream comes true!

Does the interviewer ask good questions? Why? What questions would you like to ask Maria?

DID YOU KNOW?

- There are more than seven billion people in the world. How many people live in your country?

- People are about 1cm taller in the morning than in the evening. Try to measure yourself in the morning and evening.

- Humans are the only creatures that cry when they're sad. When do you cry? When do you laugh?

- On average, girls blink twice as often as boys do. How often do you blink in one minute? How could you find out?

Perfect predators

Read this information to find out more about predators.

PREDATORS!

Predators kill and eat other animals. They have to eat meat to survive. Examples of land predators are lions, bears and wolves. Examples of predators that live in water are sharks and crocodiles.

The orca (also known as the killer whale)

Four things make the orca a perfect predator. First, they are really big and can grow up to nine metres long – that's three times bigger than a great white shark! Second, they can swim faster than other whales and dolphins. Third, they work as a team when they go hunting, so they catch more fish. And fourth, orcas are really intelligent animals and have many different tricks to catch prey.

The African lion

The African lion is not the biggest cat. It is the second biggest, after the Siberian tiger. The lion is also only the second fastest cat. The cheetah is the fastest.

Like orcas, African lions live in groups. They usually work together when they hunt. Lions can see, smell and hear very well, so they can even hunt in the dark. They are not very active and spend most of the day sleeping.

Which other predators do you know about? What do they hunt? Can you think of predators that fly? What is the smallest predator you can think of?

Be patient

Read this story about a lion.

Leona the lion

Shhh! The female lion, Leona, presses her ears flat and keeps her head low. She moves very slowly and quietly through the long grass. She does not want any of the zebras to notice she is there. Luckily, her golden coat is difficult to see in this environment. Only her eyes peep out above the grass. She crawls carefully, closer and closer. She sees a herd of zebras and looks left and right to find the perfect target.

This is hard work for Leona and she must be patient. Zebras can run quickly. Young zebras and old zebras are easier to chase because they are slower. But Leona must get very close if she wants to catch one. She is very strong and has sharp teeth, but her biggest weapon is the element of surprise.

She suddenly sees a young zebra. She jumps up and starts running. Every muscle in her body works together to give her as much power as possible. The zebras see her and make loud alarm noises. They run in different directions. The black and white stripes flashing left and right confuse Leona. The stripes seem to go in every direction. She loses her target and the young zebra manages to escape.

Leona gives up. She lies down and watches the zebras run off safely into the distance. Her heart is pumping very fast and her lungs feel like they are going to explode. Her mouth is open and she sticks her tongue out to help her cool down. This time the zebras have won. Leona must learn to be more patient and to plan her attack more carefully.

Why does Leona need to learn to be more patient?

When do you have to be patient?

Animal puzzles

Read and do these animal puzzles.

Word snake

Can you find all the animal words in this word snake?

(Hint: They share a first and last letter!)

Tigerabbitardigradelkangaroostrichamsterhinocerouspideratortoiseagle

Animal letters

Look at the word *ANIMAL* below. The letters are animals!

Can you think of animals which could be the letters of your name?

Write your name in animal letters.

A secret animal message

Can you read this message?
(Hint: Use a mirror!)

Animals are incredible. Which
animal would you like to be?

Pet puzzle

Look at the pictures. Find all the pet words in the wordsearch.

h	r	t	b	f	r	o	g
a	u	p	i	c	a	t	j
m	e	a	r	t	b	f	l
s	m	r	d	q	b	i	k
t	o	r	t	o	i	s	e
e	u	o	z	v	t	h	d
r	s	t	b	p	m	e	c
k	e	s	i	y	i	p	x

Drawing a lion

Follow these steps and learn to draw a lion!

 1   2   3   4   5   6

Weird and Wonderful

Do you know the names of the animals in the pictures?
Read the information.

No water? No problem!

Have you heard of a gerenuk? This long-necked antelope lives in the desert in East Africa. It likes to stand on two legs to eat. Gerenuks can live in very dry places because they never have to drink water.

The tiny tarsier

This little creature is a Philippine tarsier, from the island of Bohol. It is one of the smallest and cutest primates in the world. It is smaller than an adult human hand. The tarsier likes to eat insects. It has a long middle finger to dig insects out of wood. It also has a long tail and it uses this to stand upright, like a camera tripod.

The tardigrade ('water bear')

This is a tardigrade. It is a really, really small creature, less than 1 mm long. But it has been called the strongest, most durable creature on Earth. The tardigrade can survive freezing cold (-273 °C) and boiling hot temperatures (+150 °C). It can even live without food or water for thirty years!

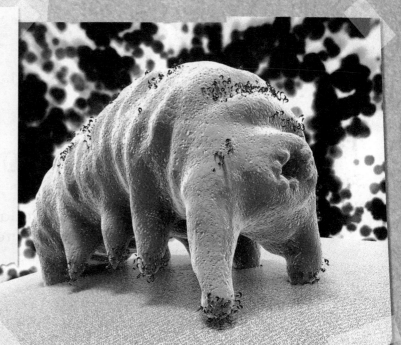

The leaf-tailed gecko

It is easy to understand why this incredible animal is called a leaf-tailed gecko. It is found in the tropical rainforests of Madagascar and relies on camouflage to survive. This means it hides by copying the shape and colour of the thing it sits on. The leaf-tailed gecko can look exactly like a leaf, so no predators will see it. It can also drop its tail if there is danger nearby, or even flatten its body, to *really* look like a leaf!

Look at the pictures. Describe the animals.

Animal activities

Read this play script based on an Aboriginal Dreaming Story.

Tiddalik the Thirsty Frog

<u>Scene 1</u>

Narrator: One hot afternoon in the Australian Outback there was a large and green and very, very thirsty frog called Tiddalik.

Tiddalik: (grumpily) It's so hot and I am so thirsty! I'll lap up the water in this water hole.

Narrator: Tiddalik drank thirstily until the water hole was dry. After that he was much fatter.

Tiddalik: I'm still thirsty. Ah! Here's a nice full stream.

Narrator: Tiddalik quickly drank all the water in the stream.

Tiddalik: I need more water. Ah. At least the lake is full of water.

Narrator: Tiddalik drank greedily until the lake was empty. After that he was much fatter than before. He could hardly move.

Tiddalik: Now I don't feel thirsty, but I do feel uncomfortable and tired.

Narrator: Tiddalik flopped down heavily and slept soundly all night.

<u>Scene 2</u>

Narrator: The next day, the Sun rose on a dry land. There was no water for the animals to drink. The animals gathered for a meeting.

Wombat: I think we should make Tiddalik laugh. That way he'll open his mouth wide and the water will flow out freely.

Narrator: The animals enthusiastically agreed that this was a good plan.

Kangaroo: (nudging Tiddalik's foot) Wake up! Wake up, Tiddalik!

Narrator: Kookaburra told his funniest joke.

Kookaburra: (laughing merrily) What is a frog's favourite time? Leap Year!

Narrator: Kookaburra fell over with laughter, yet Tiddalik didn't even smile. Then the lizards did a clumsy dance but Tiddalik just blinked. After that, Kangaroo did some high hops but Tiddalik didn't laugh.

Emu: (quietly whispering to his friends) Come on, emus, let's ruffle our feathers and peck madly at each other.

Narrator: The other animals fell about laughing at the emus. Tiddalik looked a little amused, but he didn't even smile.

All: (loudly) What shall we do?

<u>Scene 3</u>

Narrator: Later in the afternoon, an eel wiggled out from under his sleeping rock.

Eel: (bewilderedly) Where is the water? It's all gone.

Narrator: Eel crawled towards the animals gathered around Tiddalik. But the sand was hot and he couldn't crawl over it, so he tried to stand up on the end of his tail. Eel struggled awkwardly to balance. He wobbled one way and another, and bent himself in all sorts of shapes. Tiddalik stared at the eel.

How do you think the play ends?

Football for all

Listen and follow the text about a girls' football club in Kenya.

Moving the Goalposts

Football is the world's most popular sport and it is played and enjoyed by girls and boys. Football is a team sport, with eleven players in a team. It is played on a rectangular field or pitch, with goalposts at each side. The aim of the game is to try and kick the ball between the other team's goalposts.

Moving the Goalposts is the name of a sports centre in Kenya. At this centre, girls exercise to get fit and they play football. They practise ball skills and working together as a team.

On a match day you can hear the sound of girls clapping and cheering when a team scores a goal. The weather is hot and the field is a dusty brown. Many of the girls are playing without shoes and they are happy to run around and kick the ball.

Moving the Goalposts gives these girls a chance to make new friends and increase their confidence. Teamwork helps the girls to develop trust, support and respect, because everyone in the team is important and has a role to play. The best female footballers can travel and participate in international matches. The rest of the girls at Moving the Goalposts sports centre look up to these girls as role models and they strive to be like them.

Which people are sporting role models in your country? Why are they role models?

Read this poem.

Boys' Game?

'This is our side of the playground,
What are you doing here?
You want to play football?
That's a laugh!
It's a boy's game. Got it clear?'

'Actually Kev, she's pretty good,
Especially in a goal.
I saw her at the rec last night:
She was really in control.
Saved a penalty early on,
And from corner she can catch!
Dived several times
At their striker's feet –
Really kept us in the match.'

'Well in that case ...
Of course, it's actually
In goal where we're really weak.
I mean, anyone's got to be better
Than Baggs –
He couldn't play hide and seek.
Even a girl would be better than him.
Look, we've got to decide.
Let's take her on.
Hey, where's she gone ...?
Oh, she's gone back to their side.'

Eric Finney

This poem explores some of the unfairness girls may face when they play sport. How are the attitudes of the two boys different?

Is this poem funny? Why? / Why not?

These sports are really weird!

Read these descriptions of unusual sports.

Belly flopping

This is the perfect sport for people who are not good at diving. A belly flop is when you jump into a pool and land flat on your stomach and face. It makes a big splash and looks like lots of fun, but be careful as it can hurt! Each person gets three dives at a belly flopping competition. You get points for the size of the splash, for the style of your dive and even for the colour of your swimming costume.

Cheese rolling

This is an old and unusual race which started in England. All the participants start at the top of a steep hill. Someone rolls a large wheel of cheese down the hill. Then everyone runs after it. Many people slip, trip and tumble on the way down. The aim is to catch the cheese, but this doesn't often happen. The first person to cross the finish line at the bottom of the hill wins the cheese wheel.

Cardboard tube duelling

Cardboard duelling is sword fighting with cardboard tubes. Robert Easley, an American, started the duel. He wanted adults to play like children again and to be a little less serious. The rules are very easy and fun:

- Do not hit your opponent with your tube.
- Only hit your opponent's tube.
- Do not use your other hand to block or protect your tube.

The aim is to break the other person's tube, so the last person with an unbroken tube is the winner.

Which phrases describe each sport?

- Really fun?   Quite fun?   A little bit fun?
- Really interesting?   Quite interesting?   A little bit interesting?
- Really difficult?   Quite difficult?   A little bit difficult?

If It Wasn't For Tom

Listen to the story *If It Wasn't For Tom*. Read these diary pages.

Joe's diary

I love football and PE. But Tom always

makes fun of me. The new PE teacher

made Tom go running today. I felt sorry

for Tom because he was really struggling,

so I decided to help him out.

Tom's diary

I laugh at Joe. I think he's useless.

Then the teacher made me do PE with

the rest of the class and everyone laughed

at me huffing and puffing. Joe helped me

out and made me feel better. I don't pick

on him any more.

What is your opinion of Joe?

Which attitude do you admire, Joe's or Tom's? Why?

Would you have helped Tom? Why?

Be a 'Good sport'

Listen and follow the article about how to be a 'good sport'.

'That's not fair! You cheated!'

Have you ever been in a team with someone who got angry when they lost? It's not fun! It is disappointing to lose, so it's normal to feel sad. Adults don't like it either, but everyone can learn to control how they feel and act. Learning to lose without getting angry is a skill, just like riding a bike. Here is an idea to help you be a 'good sport'.

Say nice things to the other people in your team or even to the person you are playing against. For example, 'Good shot!', 'Well done!', 'That was a good try!', 'You can do it!'

Saying nice things helps you and your team to stay positive. Don't blame other people when they make a mistake. Everyone is trying their best. Instead of pointing fingers and blaming people, try to say something nice, like 'Better luck next time.'

Staying positive helps you to have fun and to learn from your mistakes.

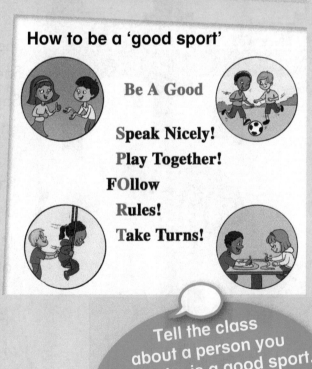

How to be a 'good sport'

Be A Good

Speak Nicely!
Play Together!
FOllow
Rules!
Take Turns!

Tell the class about a person you know who is a good sport. What do they do? How do they make others feel?

Surfing the net

Listen and follow the poem. Think about the ways in which you use the internet.

Which things does Sarah want to do on the internet?

What is she meant to do?

What do you use the internet for?

When Sarah Surfs the Internet

When Sarah surfs the internet
she starts by checking mail.
She answers all her messages
from friends in great detail.

She plays a game, or maybe two,
and watches a cartoon,
then chats with kids in places
like Rwanda and Rangoon.

She reads about her favorite bands.
She buys an MP3.
She downloads movie trailers
and she looks for stuff for free.

She reads about celebrities
and dreams of wealth and fame,
then watches music videos
and plays another game.

If you should say, 'Your time is up.
I need to use the net,'
she always whines, 'I haven't got
my homework finished yet!'

by **Kenn Nesbitt**

Let's Connect

Listen and follow the text about devices which are connected to the internet.

More and more objects around you are built with little computers in them. These computers help you connect and control these objects over the internet or via a mobile app.

Do you have a smart toothbrush?

You can buy a smart toothbrush that connects to your smartphone. It will teach you how to brush your teeth properly. It has an app that helps you turn brushing your teeth into a fun experience.

Do you have a smartwatch?

Wearing a smartwatch is like wearing a smartphone on your wrist. You can listen to music, play games, check messages and do a lot more than just tell the time on your smartwatch. Sometimes there are little sensors on the back of the watch. These measure your heart rate and how many steps you've taken.

What if your fridge could talk?

What would your refrigerator say if it could talk? This sounds like a silly question, but many technology companies are asking questions like this. Your fridge sees you put food in and take it out. It knows how much milk your family drinks and how many eggs you eat every week. Imagine if a smart fridge wrote a shopping list and ordered online for you.

Think about your home and your school. What devices are connected to the internet?

Help! I can't put my smartphone away

Read what four learners have to say about their smartphones.

Saskia

It takes me a long time to fall asleep. When I get into bed, the first thing I do is message five of my best friends. Sometimes we chat for more than an hour. When I wake up the next morning I will have a hundred notifications. Some of these notifications are messages from my friends.

Rachel

My parents always complain that I spend too much time on my phone. We often have an argument at the dinner table, because I check messages while we are eating. I don't understand why they get so angry about it. They spend more time watching television every night.

Marco

I take my phone everywhere with me, even to the bathroom! To be honest, I feel a little nervous when I don't have my phone with me because one of my friends may need to contact me. Sometimes I feel my phone vibrate, but when I check, there are no messages. It's a little strange.

Finn

I have a really cool new phone and it has loads of useful apps. Whenever I have homework, I use my phone to help me. It is easy to find the answers, so I can finish my homework really quickly. Now I have a lot more time to play games. It's great!

What do you think about what the children say? Can you give them any advice?

In the Game

Look at the cover and some pictures from the book *In the Game* by Katy Coope.

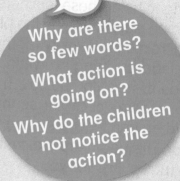

Why are there so few words?

What action is going on?

Why do the children not notice the action?

Different schools

Listen and follow the text about some learners in different schools.

Attending school in an ordinary classroom, in a normal school building is not the only way to learn. Learners all around the world are learning the same subjects as you, but in a school building that is totally different from yours.

In Bangladesh, some learners go to school on boats. It rains a lot in Bangladesh. Some areas often flood. The boat schools can float on the water and never get damaged by the floodwater. Inside the classrooms there are desks, books, a board and a teacher – just like inside your classroom. Some of the boats are in the middle of big lakes. Learners then use small boat taxis to get to school.

In India, there are many street children who are extremely poor. They cannot go to school because they don't have any money. But, there are some teachers who are trying to help. These teachers have created classrooms on the platform at a train station. Every morning, the teachers bring everything the students need for the day. There are no desks or chairs, so the children and teachers sit on the floor. They learn to read, write and do maths, just like you.

In San Fransisco, USA, there is a very different school called Brightworks. The school is in a big warehouse, and inside there are different work spaces. In one space there are drawers full of coloured paper, shelves with electronics, and tools hanging on the walls. In another workspace there are sofas and pillows on the floor. The school believes that the best way to learn is by trying it yourself. Kids who want to learn about rockets are given tools and material to build their own rocket. Teachers don't tell you what to do, but can help you if you get stuck.

Some learners attend travelling schools. This means that every semester they study in a different school, in a different country. They still learn English, maths and science, like you. But they also learn about different cultures, traditions and ways to live. These learners spend a lot of time meeting new people and learning new languages.

Compare the schools you have read about with your school.
- How are they the same?
- How are they different?

Study tips and tricks

Read about these study methods that can help to make studying easier and more interesting.

Make a mind map:

Personal goals

A mind map helps you to organise your work so that it looks nice. The more eye-catching the information looks, the easier it is to remember.

1. Write the main topic in the middle of the page.
2. Add lines for the sub-topics.
3. Then add more lines from the sub-topics, so you can write all the information in the right place.
4. Use **coloured** pencils and pictures to make it look great and help you to remember it.

Use cue cards:

Cue cards are small pieces of paper that help you to remember things.

1. Cut out your cue cards. You can use different colours for different topics. (For example: use yellow cards for geography.)
2. On the front, write a question for something you want to remember. (For example: What is the capital city of Australia?)
3. On the back, write the answer. (For example: Canberra)
4. To use your cue cards, look at the front and first try to answer the question. Then, turn the card over and check the answer.

Tokyo

What is the capital city of Japan?

Teach your friends:

Teaching is actually the best way to learn something.

1. Find a study partner or a small group to work with.
2. Divide your work into different parts.
3. Give each person one part to study.
4. After you have studied that part, teach each other.

You can even test each other to check that you have learned everything.

Use mnemonics:

Mnemonics is a big word for all the little tricks we use to help us remember something. We can make a rhyme or use our body. It is a good idea to try this when you have to remember a long list. Look at these examples:

1. To remember how many days are in each month, you can use your hands. The months that fall on your raised knuckles have 31 days. The rest of the months have 30 days, except for February.

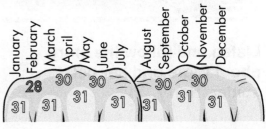

2. To remember how to spell a difficult word, you can make up a sentence.

because

Big **e**lephants **c**an **a**lways **u**nderstand **s**maller **e**lephants.

3. To remember your compass points, you can say 'Never Eat Silk Worms.'

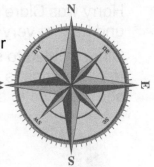

Watch videos:

We all love to watch videos. Videos are a great way to remember something. Next time you are learning something difficult, look for a video about that topic on the internet. It is amazing how many useful videos you can find.

Use your body:

Sometimes it is good to stand up and move while you are studying. You can walk and read aloud to help you remember it. Or you can use different actions to remember items in a list.

How do you study best? Which study tips and tricks will you try to use? Why?

Harry the Clever Spider at School

Listen and follow the story about Clare and her pet spider, Harry.

Harry was Clare's pet spider and he was very clever.

Clare wanted to show Harry to all her friends. On Monday she took him to school.

'We're doing minibeasts,' she told him. 'This box is just for the journey.'

But Harry didn't like his box. He hid in the corner so that Clare couldn't see him.

Harry was still hiding when they got to school.

Joanne said, 'I've got ever such a big black beetle. Look!'

Simon said, 'I've got an enormous furry caterpillar that will turn into a brilliant butterfly. Look!'

Clare said, 'I've got a huge, hairy, clever spider. Look!'

Joanne looked through one of the holes in the box and said, 'I can't see him.' No one could see Harry.

'Wait till we get inside,' said Clare.

'You'll see him when I take the lid off.'

But when they got inside, their teacher, Miss Bradley, said, 'Keep your minibeasts in their jars and boxes, children. Don't remove the lids. We can't have minibeasts running all over the classroom, can we?'

She gave out paper and pencils and put out the paint pots.

'Please observe your minibeast carefully. Then write about what you see. After that, you can draw or paint a picture of it.'

Clare looked through the holes in the lid of Harry's box, but she still couldn't see him.

She said, 'Please Miss Bradley, I can't see Harry with the lid on.'

But Miss Bradley wasn't listening. She had lost her glasses. She was always losing them! She said, 'Get on with your work everyone, while I look for my glasses.'

Clare opened the lid to peep at Harry, who jumped out … and scuttled away!

Clare had never seen him move so fast.

'See,' said Joanne, looking into the box. 'It's empty.'

'You were fibbing,' said Simon. 'You haven't got a clever spider. You haven't got a spider at all!'

Clare was upset. Where was Harry? Miss Bradley was upset. Where were her glasses? She said, 'I can't see without my glasses. Children, please help me look for them.'

Everybody started looking for Miss Bradley's glasses, except Clare. She was looking for Harry.

She looked on her table. 'There he is!' But it was a splash of black paint. She looked on the next table. 'There he is!' But it was another splash of black paint.

9

Then Clare looked again, more closely. She saw a trail … leading down the table leg, across the floor and up the wall, to the ceiling.

10

11

'There's Harry!' yelled Clare. 'There's my clever spider!'

Everybody was looking at Harry. Miss Bradley was furious.

'Clare, I told you to keep your minibeast INSIDE its box!'

Clare said, 'Sorry, Miss Bradley, but I think Harry's seen something.'

Harry was bungee jumping. Down he went … then up again, just like a yo-yo.

Then he went down behind the cupboard. Harry had seen something ...

12

13

Very Clever Spider

… Miss Bradley's glasses!

'You really are a clever spider,' said Miss Bradley.

'He's very clever,' said Clare. 'Look at him now.'

Written by Julia Jarman and illustrated by Charlie Fowkes.

Is *Harry the Clever Spider at School* a good title for the story? Why? / Why not?

Which minibeast would you like to show the class? Why?

Let's communicate

Look at the pictures and read the information.

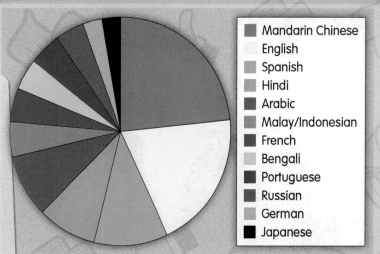

The information in the pie chart shows the most widely spoken languages in the world.

- Which language is spoken by the most people in the world?
- Which language is spoken by the second most people in the world?

Legend:
- Mandarin Chinese
- English
- Spanish
- Hindi
- Arabic
- Malay/Indonesian
- French
- Bengali
- Portuguese
- Russian
- German
- Japanese

Fun facts

- This is the shortest English sentence that uses *all* 26 letters of the alphabet: *The quick brown fox jumps over the lazy dog.*

- Write 'SWIMS' in capital letters. Now turn it upside down. What can you see?

- *Typewriter* is the longest English word that can be made using the letters in the top row of a keyboard (Q W E R T Y U I O P).

  How many other words can you make from those letters?

Every picture tells a story

Communication helps us to solve problems. Mojo and Weeza have a problem to solve in this book.

Look at the cover.

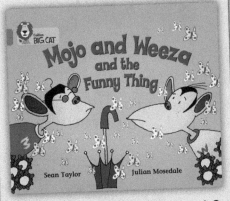

What is the title of the book?

Who wrote and illustrated the book?

What do you think the book is about?

Describe the characters.

Mojo and Weeza and the Funny Thing

Listen and follow the story about Mojo and Weeza.

Mojo and Weeza found a funny thing.

Mojo said, 'I know what it is! It's a **boat**.'

But the boat didn't float.

Weeza said, 'I know what it is! It's a **rocket**.'

They counted … 10…9 …8…7…6…5…4…3… 2…1…BLAST OFF!

But the rocket didn't take off.

Mojo said, 'I know what it is! It's a **parachute**.'

He climbed up a tree and jumped.

But the parachute didn't work.

Weeza said, 'I know what it is! It's a **tent**.'

He lay down under it, but the funny thing was too small.

Then it started raining and that was when Mojo said, 'I KNOW WHAT IT IS!'

Mojo turned the funny thing around and it filled with rain.

Then he got in. Mojo said, 'It's a **bath**.'

Weeza said, 'Of course it is!'

And that's what the funny thing was … well, sort of.

What problem did Mojo and Weeza need to solve?

Did they solve the problem? How do you know?

How do you communicate?

Listen and follow the text.

Sign language

Some people cannot hear. They use a special language to communicate. They use hand signals to make words and sentences. This language is called sign language. Here are some common expressions in sign language.

happy

sad

angry

hungry

tired

excited

embarrassed

frightened

confused

Try to communicate with your friend using sign language.

Braille

Some people cannot see. They learn to read the Braille alphabet with their fingers. Braille letters are made by making raised dots on a page. A person reads Braille by moving their fingers over the dots.

Secret codes

A code is used to send someone a secret message. It can be made from a set of letters, numbers or symbols. Read about these codes.

This is the machine used to make the sound.

Morse code

Morse code uses 'dots' (short) and 'dashes' (long) to send a message. You can use light or sound to send a Morse code message. It is useful for sending a short message over a long distance.

Can you say 'hello' to your friend in Morse code? You can say 'beep' for a dot and 'beeeep' for a dash.

This is the code:

Number codes

You can make your own code by changing each letter to a number. Look at this table:

A	B	C	D	E	F	G	H	I	J	K	L	M
2	12	11	20	4	15	19	5	8	14	25	7	16

N	O	P	Q	R	S	T	U	V	W	X	Y	Z
9	22	10	21	3	13	6	1	23	18	26	24	17

What does this message say?

18-4-7-7   20-22-9-4!

24-22-1   13-22-7-23-4-20   6-5-4   11-22-20-4.

Now make your own number code and write a message to your friend.

Letter codes

You could change each letter to another letter instead of numbers.
Look at this table:

A	B	C	D	E	F	G	H	I	J	K	L	M
G	X	S	E	O	W	A	I	L	T	D	Z	N
N	O	P	Q	R	S	T	U	V	W	X	Y	Z
K	P	J	Q	C	R	B	U	Y	F	V	M	H

What does this message say?

SPEO-XROGDLKA   LB   WYK!

Now make your own letter code and write a message to your friend.

Symbol codes

If you want to be creative, you can use symbols.
Look at this table:

A	B	C	D	E	F	G	H	I	J	K	L	M
❖	✂	▢	➤	✳	✗	▼	◗	✿	❮	✛	🐛	♥
N	O	P	Q	R	S	T	U	V	W	X	Y	Z
✓	○	✪	☞	◆	❄	★	▲	⇨	✈	✉	→	✏

What does this message say?

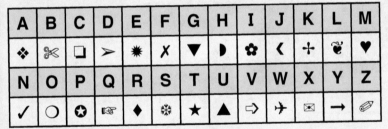

Now use your own symbols to write a coded message.

Crack these codes

1 The hippos eat yellow and red eggs, honey and purple pears yay!

2 rewoT leffiE eht nees evah dna siraP ot neeb evah I.

3 Ip ltifkjew tdablmkaisnbgz arnydp lwissktpeynmicnbgt.

4 MtohjeoyaunsdeWieteazsaafbiantdhainnutmhberrealilna.

Number codes: Well done! You solved the code.

Letter codes: Code-breaking is fun!

Symbol codes: Try, try and try again. Practice makes perfect!

Crack the codes:
1 They are happy. (This code uses the first letter of each word to make a new message. You could also use the second or third letter of each word.)
2 I have been to Paris and have seen the Eiffel Tower. (This code is written backwards.)
3 I like talking and listening. (This code uses every second letter to spell out the words. It starts with the first letter.)
4 Mojo and Weeza find an umbrella. They use it as a bath in the rain. (First, read every second letter, starting with 'M'. Then read the letters in between, starting with 'J'.)

Marvellous Milly Makes Her First Speech

Listen and follow the story about Milly and her first day at a new school.

Milly felt nervous about moving to Mexico. She was scared to join a new school and make new friends. Being a shy and quiet girl she knew she would find it difficult to talk to new people.

On her first day in her new school, Miss Garcia said, 'Hello Milly. Welcome to our class. I'm sure you will be very happy here.' Then Miss Garcia turned to the rest of the class and said, 'Raise your hand if you have ever been to Canada.' No one raised their hand. 'Milly is from Canada.' Then she looked at Milly and said, 'After lunch, you can stand up and tell us a bit about yourself and your country.' During lunch time, Milly was very nervous. She was afraid of public speaking.

After lunch, Miss Garcia called Milly to the front of the classroom. Milly tried to stand up, but her legs wouldn't move. She tried to smile, but her mouth wouldn't move. 'What if I become a statue and am stuck in this chair forever?' she wondered. Then the girl next to Milly took her hand and walked with her to the front of the classroom. Milly smiled. 'I can do this,' she thought.

At first, Milly's voice sounded like a little mouse squeaking, but as she spoke, she became more confident. She started telling the class all about her family. She told them about Canada and her old school. She told them about her hobbies and funny stories about her friends.

Finally the bell rang. Milly had talked for the whole lesson. Her new classmates nicknamed her 'Marvellous Milly' because of her marvellous stories. She has many friends now at her new school, and is very happy with her new Mexican life.

Public speaking

Public speaking is when you stand up in front of a crowd of people and make a speech. Many people feel nervous when they have to make a speech. Sometimes they speak softly or too fast. Sometimes their hands shake or their knees tremble. Sometimes their face goes red or they can't speak at all.

Other people love public speaking. When they stand up in front of a group of people they speak slowly, clearly and loudly. They remember all their words. They use expressive body language and are very interesting. Public speaking is an important skill to learn.

How do you feel when you speak in front of a group of people?

Why is public speaking a useful skill to learn?

Hunting for treasure

Read these articles about treasure hunts and look at the pictures.

The world's largest treasure hunt

Have you heard about geocaching? (Say *jee-oh-cash-ing*.) It is a fun game that anyone can play ... anytime, anywhere! Okay, maybe you can't play while you are at school, but you can ask your parents to play with you over the weekend.

Geocaching is like one huge treasure hunt. It happens all around the world. In fact, there are more than two million treasures hidden right now! Maybe there are even some near to where you live.

To find the treasure, you need to download the app, or visit the website. If you search for 'geocaching' online, you can find it easily. Then you can see a map and follow the map to find the treasure.

When you find the treasure, you can sign the logbook. This is a tiny book with a list of the names of everyone who has found treasure in the same place. You can keep the treasure you find, but you must put a new treasure in the box for the next person to find. Good luck!

> Would you like to join *The Amazing Race*? Why?

The Amazing Race

Have you watched *The Amazing Race*? It is a reality television show. In this show, teams race around the world. They are on a global treasure hunt. The teams need to find clues, solve problems and travel to many different places to find the treasure.

Each team has two people. They travel through different countries and use many different types of transport. They travel by aeroplane, helicopter and hot air balloon to fly overseas. They travel by bus, train, bicycle, car and taxi to ride over land. They travel by boat, ship and rafts to cross over water.

Sometimes the clues are easy, but other times they are difficult. Often you need to ask local people to help you. If you want to win *The Amazing Race*, you have to be smart, fit and friendly.

Metal detecting

Do you know what a metal detector is? It is a machine that beeps when it is near metal. Metal things can be anything from bottle caps, paperclips or old nails, to special coins or expensive jewellery.

Some people use metal detectors to try and find treasure. They walk up and down a beach, a garden or a large area of land looking for valuable metal objects.

In 1977, a man found the largest piece of gold in the world. It is called the Mojave Nugget.

In 2007, a British father and son were metal detecting together. They found a treasure chest full of gold and silver.

Imagine finding treasure! What treasure would you like to find, and where?

In 2012, a young boy found a real meteorite. This is a rock that comes from space. Wow!

What is a map?

Read the information and the poem about maps.

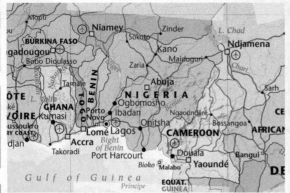

Maps

Maps are diagrams that show our world on a flat surface. Everything on a map is smaller than it actually is in real life. You can find maps of very large areas like a country or even the whole world. You can find maps of smaller areas like a city or a suburb. You can also find maps of much smaller areas, like your school or a shopping centre.

Some maps show natural things such as rivers, lakes, mountains, forests and deserts. Other maps show things built by people, such as roads, bridges, houses, hospitals and schools.

A person who draws maps is called a cartographer. A long time ago, explorers drew what they saw while travelling to new places. When they were home again, cartographers used their information to draw a map. Now people use computers and satellites to help them make maps. Cities are always changing, so people need to check that the information on their map is up-to-date.

Making Maps

I love to make maps!
I think it's great fun,
Making the boundaries
And then one by one
Putting in railroads.
And each river bend,
And the tiny towns
Where little roads end.
I draw in the mountains,
And often a lake,
And I've even had
Long bridges to make!
I like to do highways.
And when they are drawn
I dream that they take me
Where I've never gone.

Elaine V. Emans

What maps have you used?
What types of information do you find on maps?
Why do we need maps?

Mojo and Weeza and the New Hat

Listen, look and follow the story.

Mojo and Weeza looked very smart.

Mojo had new shoes and Weeza had a new hat.

Then there was a gust of wind and Weeza's hat blew away.

'My new hat!' said Weeza. 'It's gone!'

'Where to?' asked Mojo.

Weeza looked around.

'There! By those rocks!' he said.

But it wasn't Weeza's new hat.

It was a pan.

'There! Up that tree!' said Mojo.

But it wasn't Weeza's new hat.
It was a bird's nest.

'There! Down that hole!'
said Mojo.

5

But it wasn't Weeza's new hat.
It was a turtle.
Weeza sat down by the mud hole.
Then Mojo saw Weeza's new hat.
'There!' he shouted.

6

Both of them sploshed through the mud to get the hat.

7

'That's better,' said Weeza, as he put his new hat back on.
The two of them looked smart again … well, almost.

8

Have you ever lost something? How did you find it? Describe what happened.

Where on Earth?

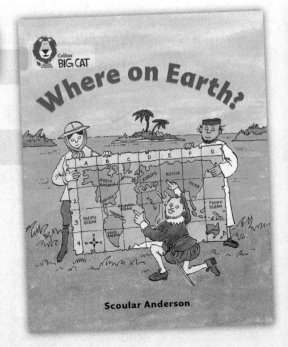

Scoular Anderson

Look at this book cover. Answer these questions.

- Who is the author of the book?
- What do you think the book is about?

Listen to this information about explorers from the book *Where on Earth?*

Look at the pictures and map while you listen.

Polynesians

Many thousands of years ago, people from South-east Asia began to make long journeys across the sea. They were some of the first explorers to make sea voyages of discovery. The places they found were often just specks of land scattered across the ocean.

Where on earth did they go?

Clue: Go to G3.

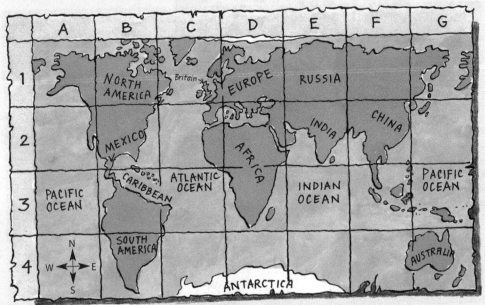

Answer: The Pacific Ocean

These sailors explored the Pacific Ocean without maps or equipment. Today, their descendants live on the Polynesian Islands, like Tonga, Tahiti and Hawaii or on larger islands like New Zealand.

The first sailors, like the Polynesians, had no maps or equipment to guide them.

They watched the pattern of clouds and waves.

They looked at the positions of the Sun, Moon and stars.

Seeing sea birds, seaweed and sea creatures often meant land was near.

(**descendants**: people living now who are related to people living in the past)

Which other early explorers have you heard about?

Where did they go and what did they do?

Take a break

Look at the pictures. What do you think *Take a break* means? Read the texts. Then listen to them.

A siesta

Siesta means 'nap' in Spanish. In Spain it is common for shops to close at lunch time and for people to take a long lunch break. This lunch break is usually between 2pm and 4pm. Many people believe that all Spanish people have lunch and take a siesta every day, but that is not true. There are different reasons why shops are closed during this time. One reason is because it is very hot in Spain, and people don't want to go outside when it is so hot. Another reason is that family is very important, so many people go home to eat with their family. After lunch some people do take a short nap. At 4pm, people go back to work and shops open their doors again. It may sound strange, but this is very normal in Spain.

Carlos takes siestas

This is Carlos. He lives in Malaga, in the south of Spain. Carlos is a salesman at a clothing store, in the centre of town. He works from Tuesday to Saturday. His day starts at 06:00, when he wakes up. He has a shower, eats breakfast, and then catches a bus to work. He starts work at 08:00, but the store only opens to the public at 08:30.

Every afternoon, Carlos closes the shop at 14:00 and walks to his mother's house. There, he eats lunch with his parents. His dad usually makes sandwiches for everyone. They talk about what has happened in the morning and the news on TV. Before he goes back to work, he has a short siesta.

Carlos opens the shop again at 16:00. For the rest of the day, he helps customers find clothes in the store. At 19:30, there are not many people in the store, and Carlos starts to count how much money people have spent at his store. At 20:00, the store closes and Carlos catches the bus back home. He enjoys his job because he meets a lot of interesting people.

Stretch

The World Health Organisation says that people should exercise for at least 30 minutes every day. But in some countries, like Japan, this is very difficult. People spend a long time sitting in traffic or sitting at work. If people do not get enough exercise, they can become very sick.

Some companies have created compulsory exercise breaks, to help all their staff get more exercise. After lunch, one online shopping company makes everyone stand up and stretch. First they stretch to the right, and then to the left. They also have to look up at the ceiling, then down at their toes. These exercises help to stretch muscles in the arms, back and neck. It also increases blood flow through the body, which is very important.

Do you have time in the day to relax? Describe your day.

Takumi needs time

Takumi works in Tokyo and it takes him 55 minutes to get to work. At work he sits at a desk for four hours until lunch time. At lunch time he walks downstairs to the cafeteria and eats lunch with his co-workers. After lunch he goes back to his desk, where he works until 8pm. Sometimes he will get a coffee at 5pm to help him concentrate. After work, he spends another 50 minutes getting home. When he gets home it is late and he must cook dinner. Takumi says he has no time to exercise.

Summer holidays

Listen first, and then read this poem about the horses' holiday fun in the sun.

Horses' Holiday

Hooray! Hooray!

It's the horses' holiday!

They come by coach, they come by car,

They come from far away.

They come from Horsey-lulu Land

And Paddock-on-the-Hay.

Some are black and some are brown,

And some are dapple gray.

This one's tail is tied up

In a very pretty way.

This one wears a sun hat,

Which he bought on Saturday.

Some lounge by the poolside

With drinks upon a tray.

Some set off on picnics,

With hampers stuffed with hay.

The braver ones hire water skis

And zoom around the bay,

Splashing all the lilos

And making lots of spray.

The babies splash in rock pools
And play and play and play.
Their mums sit round on beach mats,
And neigh and neigh and neigh.
The old ones stroll along the pier
And dream of yesterday.

The little ones want ice creams,
And are lining up to pay.
This one writes some postcards
To his nice old Aunty May,
And his granny and his grandpa,
And his little cousin Kay.

Each evening on the campsite,
They have a horse DJ.
He is the very best around
(At least, that's what they say).
He wants them up and dancing
And they're longing to obey!

At midnight, there are fireworks,
A dazzling display.
But nothing lasts for ever.
The time has ticked away.
The holiday is over,
To everyone's dismay.
They hug and kiss each other,
In a sorry sort of way.
Will they all come back next year?
'**You bet we will!**' they say.

Which activities in the poem would you like to do? Why? Which activities wouldn't you like to do? Why?

Let's travel

Read the texts to find out about different holidays.

Travel to Spain for *La Tomatina*

Spain is famous for having fantastic fun festivals. The Spanish often play traditional music and dance when they celebrate. One of Spain's most famous festivals, *La Tomatina*, is held in August each year. It is the world's biggest food fight because each year more than 40,000 people join this festival. They throw over 150,000 tomatoes at each other, so they get very dirty! The fight only lasts an hour, but it is great fun. If you are looking for fun and don't mind getting dirty then this is the holiday for you.

Travel to Kenya to see wild animals

If you go on an African safari, you will see lions, giraffes, elephants and many other wild animals. You'll see animals both near and far while you are travelling around in an open vehicle. Bring your binoculars so you can zoom in on the animal action. If you are lucky, you can experience the great migration where millions of animals travel together to find food and water for winter. But be careful, wild animals can be dangerous! If warm weather and wild animals are what you are looking for then this is the holiday for you.

Travel to Mongolia for a camel trek

If you go to Mongolia, you can do a camel trek and live like a nomad in the desert. A nomad is a person who doesn't live in the same place for a long time – they move from place to place. During the day, you will travel many hours by camel. At night, you will sleep in tents and be able to see hundreds of stars. If a quiet and peaceful holiday in the desert is what you are looking for, then this is the holiday for you.

Holiday at home

Maybe for you, the perfect holiday is a relaxing one at home. You can wake up late in the morning, relax, play games, watch television or meet your friends whenever you want to. Is this the holiday for you?

There is an English name for a person who sits on the couch and watches television every day ... we call them a *couch potato*!

What kind of holiday would you most/least like to go on?

What things do you like / not like doing during the holidays? Why?

Where shall we go?

What shall we do?

Look at the pictures and read about these different holiday destinations.

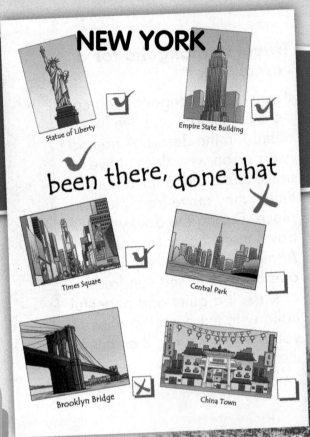

NEW YORK

Statue of Liberty ✓

Empire State Building ✓

been there, done that ✗

Times Square ✓

Central Park ☐

Brooklyn Bridge ✗

China Town ☐

Gran

Hi Gran! We finally have reception again!

Hello Bo! How's was your trip to Drakensberg?

It was GREAT!

The mountains were lovely, and camping was a lot of fun! We all pitched our tents on the first day.

What did you do there?

We woke up early every morning to go hiking. We also went fishing and swimming. And at night we sat around the campfire telling stories.

That sounds fantastic!

Yes it was! I'll tell you about it when I'm back home!

See you tomorrow! Bye!

I look forward to hearing all about it! Bye Bo!

Elephant Shower in Thailand!

June 25th

Today we went to an elephant camp. The elephants at this camp are retired. They used to work in a forest, pulling heavy logs out of the forest. But now they spend most of the day in the water playing. One elephant squirted water out of her trunk and gave me and my brother a shower! It was so funny. We also got a chance to feed the elephants bananas, which is their favourite snack!

Afterwards we went to the elephant nursery, where we saw baby elephants. They are so cute! It was a great day!

Do you ever write about your holidays? Have you ever written a blog about your holiday? What kind of holiday would/ wouldn't you enjoy? Why?

Rising above the challenge

Read this information.

The Olympic Games is an event that happens every four years, either in the winter or the summer. It is held in a different country each time. At each Olympics, the best athletes from around the world gather to compete in different sports competitions. These athletes, also knows as competitors, have to work incredibly hard to be selected for their country's Olympic team. Each competitor dreams of winning and breaking a world record!

Olympic Heroes

Going for gold

The first modern Olympic Games were held in Athens, Greece, in 1896. American James Connolly was the first medal winner. He won the medal for the triple jump.

Did you know? The early champions' medals were not gold but silver!

The first Winter Olympics were held in 1924. Since then, many of the world's top athletes have gone for Olympic gold. But some have to fight harder than most to become Olympic champions.

Read about these competitors who had to work even harder than normal because of the challenges they faced.

Brave beginners

These men were the first to come from a hot, sunny country to compete in a winter sport. At home, they had to practise on tracks and sandy beaches.

They had to borrow bobsleighs from other teams for the Winter Olympics.

They crashed on a run, but walked on to the finish line as the crowd cheered.

The Jamaican bobsleigh team.

The Jamaican bobsleigh team at the 1988 Winter Olympics in Canada.

Winning wheels

This woman was born with a condition which meant she couldn't walk or run. Being in a wheelchair didn't stop her becoming a great athlete and champion. She entered her first wheelchair race when she was 13 and won her first medal in the Paralympic Games six years later.

Tanni Grey-Thompson races to the finish in her orange wheelchair.

She had to stop training to have an operation on her spine, but went on to win four gold medals in the 1992 Games. She took part in five Paralympic Games and won a total of 16 medals, including 11 golds.

Future champions

Every Olympic Games brings new champions. All have trained hard and some have overcome illness, disability or prejudice to win gold. There'll be many more Olympic heroes in the future.

Have you watched the Olympic Games? Which are your favourite events? Why?

First Day

It was Flynn's first day at school and he was feeling a bit nervous.

'I'm a bit nervous,' he said to his mum and dad.

'What if I get something wrong?'

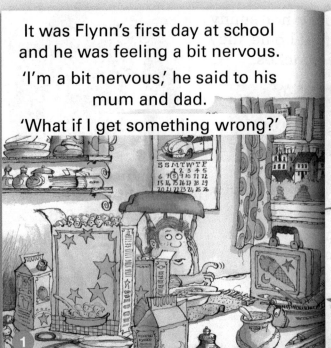

Flynn's mum and dad smiled. 'Don't worry, Flynn,' they said. 'Lots of people get things wrong on their first day.'

Police officer Julie Nicks gave a robber an ice cream on her first day.

Rod Hod, the builder, built a house upside down on his first day.

Ned Mutton, the farm worker, tried to milk the chickens on his first day.

Rose Trellis, the gardener, cut the flowers instead of the grass on her first day.

Shirley Curly, the hairdresser, used the wrong scissors on her first day.

Anna Conda, the zookeeper, tried to sweep out the shark tank on her first day.

Raci Pastree, the cook, put jam in the sausage rolls on his first day.

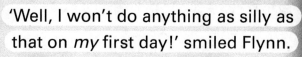

'Well, I won't do anything as silly as that on *my* first day!' smiled Flynn.

'Of course you won't ...' said Mum and Dad ...

...'but you might want to change out of your pyjamas before you go to school!'

Did anything go wrong on your first day at school?
If you get something wrong, what do you usually do?

Guinness World Records

Read about the Guinness World Records.

The Guinness World Records started in 1955. It is a list of records from around the world. For example, the *tallest* man, the *longest* hair or the *fastest* runner. Many people work very hard to break a Guinness World Record. Some people even try some crazy and ridiculous things to be original and achieve a world record!

World's longest human mattress domino

2,019 people stood with mattresses. Then one by one the people fell over onto one another to break this record. It took just over 11 minutes for everyone to fall over.

Q: On average, did it take a person more or less than one second to fall over?

Most snails on face

11-year-old Fin Keleher from the USA put 43 live snails on his face to break this record.

Q: How would you feel if you had to do this?

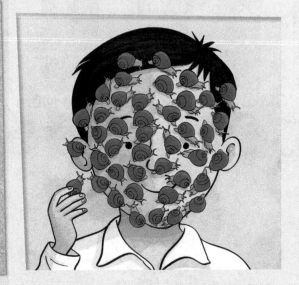

Most toilet seats broken by a person's head in one minute

This record is held by Kevin Shelley from the USA. He broke 46 toilet seats with his head, in one minute.

Q: Would you like to try and break this record? Why?

Most people brushing their teeth at the same time

In Bhubaneshwar, India, about 26,400 students brushed their teeth for two minutes to break the record.

Q: Do you think this was an easy record to break or not? Why?

World's largest sandwich

The largest sandwich in the world weighed 2,467.5 kg. That's as heavy as an elephant! It was made in Michigan, USA.

Q: How many people do you think were needed to carry the sandwich?

World's tallest and shortest people

Sultan Kösen (from Turkey) is the tallest man in the world. He is 246 cm. Chandra Dangi (from Nepal) is the shortest man in the world. He is 54.6 cm.

Q: What is the difference between their heights?

Which Guinness World Record would you like to break?

Which Guinness World Record could your class try to break?

William Collins' dream of knowledge for all began with the publication of his first book in 1819.
A self-educated mill worker, he not only enriched millions of lives, but also founded a flourishing publishing house. Today, staying true to this spirit, Collins books are packed with inspiration, innovation and practical expertise. They place you at the centre of a world of possibility and give you exactly what you need to explore it.

Collins. Freedom to teach.

An imprint of HarperCollins*Publishers*
The News Building
1 London Bridge Street
London SE1 9GF

HarperCollins*Publishers*
1st Floor, Watermarque Building
Ringsend Road
Dublin 4
Ireland

Browse the complete Collins catalogue at
www.collins.co.uk

© HarperCollins*Publishers* Limited 2021

10 9 8 7 6 5 4 3

ISBN 978-0-00-836914-9

British Library Cataloguing in Publication Data
A catalogue record for this publication is available from the British Library.

Authors Robert Kellas, Sandy Gibbs, Kathryn Gibbs
Publisher Elaine Higgleton
Series editor Daphne Paizee
Product manager: Lucy Cooper
Development editor Cait Hawkins
Project manager: Lucy Hobbs
Proof reader: Jo Kemp
Cover design by Gordon MacGilp
Cover artwork: HarperCollins *Publishers* Ltd © 2007 (Kes Gray)
Internal design by Ken Vail Graphic Design
Typesetting by QBS Learning
Illustrations by QBS Learning
Production controller: Lyndsey Rogers
Printed and Bound in the UK using 100% Renewable Electricity at CPI Group (UK) Ltd

Text acknowledgements

The publishers gratefully acknowledge the permissions granted to reproduce copyright material in the book. Every effort has been made to contact the holders of copyright material, but if any have been inadvertently overlooked, the Publisher will be pleased to make the necessary arrangements at the first opportunity.

The poem "Boys' Game" by Eric Finney, published in Football Fever by John Foster, Oxford University Press, copyright © 2000. Used with kind permission from Mrs Sheilagh Finney; and the poem "When Sarah Surfs the Internet" © 2007 by Kenn Nesbitt. Reprinted from "Revenge of the Lunch Ladies" with the permission of Meadowbrook Press.

HarperCollins*Publishers* Limited for extracts and artwork from:

If It Wasn't For Tom by Catherine MacPhail, illustrated by Francesco Ghersina, text © 2013 Catherine MacPhail. *In the Game* by Katy Coope, illustrated by Katy Coope, text © 2012 Katy Coope. *Harry the Clever Spider at School* by Julia Jarman, illustrated by Charlie Fowkes, text © 2007 Julia Jarman. *Mojo and Weeza and the Funny Thing* by Sean Taylor, illustrated by Julian Mosedale, text © 2005 Sean Taylor. *Mojo and Weeza and the New Hat* by Sean Taylor, illustrated by Julian Mosedale, text © 2007 Sean Taylor. *Where on Earth?* by Scoular Anderson, illustrated by Scoular Anderson, text © 2005 Scoular Anderson. *Horses' Holiday* by Kaye Umansky, illustrated by Ainslie Macleod, text © 2005 Kaye Umansky. *Olympic Heroes* by Jillian Powell, text © 2012 Jillian Powell. *First Day* by Kes Gray, illustrated by Korky Paul, text © 2007 Kes Gray.

Photo acknowledgements

The publishers wish to thank the following for permission to reproduce photographs. Every effort has been made to trace copyright holders and to obtain their permission for the use of copyright materials. The publishers will gladly receive any information enabling them to rectify any error or omission at the first opportunity.

(t = top, c = centre, b = bottom, r = right, l = left)

p4t Monkey Business Images/Shutterstock, p4b Phuong D. Nguyen/Shutterstock, p5t betto rodrigues/Shutterstock, p5c Aman Ahmed Khan/Shutterstock, p5b Africa Studio/Shutterstock, p6t Paul Zimmerman/Getty, p6b Denis Pogostin/Shutterstock, p7t White House Photo/Alamy, p7c ZUMA Press, Inc./Alamy, p7b C Flanigan/Getty, pp6-7 (background) Triff/Shutterstock, p9t SpeedKingz/Shutterstock, p9b Phuong D. Nguyen/Shutterstock, p10 NelzTabcharani316/Shutterstock, p11t underworld/Shutterstock, p11b Simon Eeman/Shutterstock, p12 AfriPics.com/Alamy, p12 (background) UDKOV ANDREY/Shutterstock, p14l Vitaly Titov/Shutterstock, p14r Volodymyr Burdiak/Shutterstock, p15t Giovanni Cancemi/Shutterstock, p15b Valt Ahyppo/Shutterstock, p18t/b TONY KARUMBA/Getty, pp18-19 (background) THPStock/Shutterstock, p20b 1000 Words/Shutterstock, p24b (also inset on p3) Tom Wang/Shutterstock, p24 (background) gst/Shutterstock, p25 Macrovector/Shutterstock, Ronnie21/Shutterstock, AVA Bitter/Shutterstock, p25 (background) stockchairatgfx/Shutterstock, p26t leungchopan/Shutterstock, p26cl SpeedKingz/Shutterstock, p26cr Fabiana Ponzi/Shutterstock, p26b MIA Studio/Shutterstock, p26 (background) Maxx-Studio/Shutterstock, p28t Jonas Gratzer/Getty, p28b Des Willie/Alamy, p29t Melia Robinson/Tech Insider, p29b Iakov Filimonov/Shutterstock, p30b Monkey Business Images/Shutterstock, p30 (background) Route55/Shutterstock, p31tl Pretty Vectors/Shutterstock, p31tr Sergey Mastepanov/Shutterstock, p31cl GagliardiImages/Shutterstock, p31br Rawpixel.com/Shutterstock, p35 (fox) Blue Planet Earth/Shutterstock, p35 (swim) StudioIcon/Shutterstock, p35 (background) ivector/Shutterstock, p36 (background) ElenaBukharina/Shutterstock, p37b wavebreakmedia/Shutterstock, p38t Anneka/Shutterstock, pp40-41 (background) Marko Poplasen/Shutterstock, p42t Aigars Reinholds/Shutterstock, p42tc Lasse Hendriks/Shutterstock, p42bc/b CBS Photo Archive/Getty, pp42-43 (background) phoelixDE/Shutterstock, p43t Vasilii Aleksandrov/Shutterstock, p43cr Olin Feuerbacher/Shutterstock, p43bl LEON NEAL /Getty, p43br Adwo/Shutterstock, p44tl © Collins Bartholomew Ltd 2017, p44tr david pearson/Alamy, p44bl © Collins Bartholomew Ltd 2017, p44br 4kclips/Shutterstock, pp44-45 (background) Kolonko/Shutterstock, p45b © Collins Bartholomew Ltd 2017, p50 (also inset) ProStockStudio/Shutterstock, p51t Andrey_Popov/Shutterstock, p51b (also inset on p3) 2p2play/Shutterstock, pp52-43 (background) Niko28/Shutterstock, p54t Iakov Filimonov/Shutterstock, p54b Robcartorres/Shutterstock, p55t haraldmuc/Shutterstock, p55c Rod Savely/Shutterstock, p55b Creativa Images/Shutterstock, pp56-57 (background and also inset on p3) Chantal de BrWijne/Shutterstock, p57tr Milkovasa/Shutterstock, p57tl hangingpixels/Shutterstock, p57b Ana Flasker/Shutterstock, p58tr vivairina1 /Shutterstock, p58cr ullsteinbild/TopFoto, p58cl Topical Press Agency/Stringer/Getty, p58b Gareth Copley/PA Images, p59t/r AFP/Getty, p59bl Gareth Copley/PA Images, p62t Rose-Mel/Shutterstock

With thanks to the following teachers and schools for reviewing materials in development: Hawar International School; Melissa Brobst, International School of Budapest; Niki Tzorzis, Pascal Primary School Lemessos.